A MONK'S VIEW OF LIFE

SHARAM

EDITED BY
Shahed & Nafiseh

TALIA

A MONK'S VIEW OF LIFE
SHARAM

Edited by: Shahed & Nafiseh
Paperback 1st Edition
Published in 2021 by:

Talia, Friends of Existence, Inc.
Website: www.taliafriends.org
Email: talia@taliafriends.org

Copyright © 2021 by Talia, Friends of Existence, Inc.
ISBN 978-0-9600047-3-7

All rights reserved.

No part of this book may be reproduced, stored in a retrieval system, or transmitted in any form or by any means, electronic, mechanical, photocopying, recording or otherwise, without the prior written permission of the publisher.

Many thanks to Melina H, Stefan Hoelscher, and Chris Pearson for their invaluable help.
Cover Art & Paintings: Sharam
Page Layout & Book Design: No Mind Design

More Books
by Sharam

Order now on:
TaliaFriends.org

Clarity for Your Day

Don't Beat Yourself Up

You Are Your Happiness

The Book of Existence
Part One

Mysticism
The Psychology of Love

Happiness
The Essence of Your Being

Decoding Love
Understanding is Compassion

From Negativity to Joy

The Power of Let-Go

Happiness
The Name of Our Soul

Everything in this universe is total love. We just have to discover the love. In order to discover love, we have to work on ourselves. We have to understand and meditate, put time and energy into it. We cannot expect anyone to have love if they have never worked on themselves—if they have never tried to gain a deeper understanding of themselves. But if we have love, everything around us becomes soft. When we have love, people become nice around us. Everywhere we go, we encounter softness. People who have love will recognize your love. They will respond to it and love you back. Even people who don't have love will become softer and more respectful of you. Love is everything.

Love is at the border of the soul. There are many stages to get to the domain of the soul, or enlightenment. The last stage is love. We feel love when we are with an enlightened being or with anyone who has reached this final stage of love. But we cannot be with an enlightened or loving person all the time. So in the meantime, we meditate. Meditation helps us to develop love on our own.

The love and awareness that we gain through meditation bring deep understanding. Then, this deeper understanding brings even more love and awareness to us. Understanding is the result of love and awareness.

Wanting love is not the same as having love. If someone has love, they don't want love anymore. Love pours out of them; others feel it and return that love back to them. The person with love has a loving relationship with everyone. It comes from the heart. To have love and to want love are totally different phenomena.

We can never blame anyone for not loving us. If *we* have love, others will love us. Love happens in the fourth chakra. If we are in the lower chakras, the first through third, we cannot expect others to love us. It is like going to the kitchen and looking for a shower. If we are not in the fourth chakra, we are not where love is. If you want a shower, go to the bathroom; if you want love, go to the fourth chakra and love will be everywhere.

Do you know what it means when someone is selfish? It means that person hasn't been loved, and by being selfish, they are trying to love themselves. They want love, they just don't know how to go about it. There is nothing wrong with selfishness; the only problem is selfish people cannot really love. If you love yourself, you love everyone. Then there is no reason to be selfish.

On the surface, we are what we have been taught by society, our parents, and our environment. For example, one person has been taught that everyone is his enemy, so, he has become closed. Someone else has been taught that he has to defend himself all the time, so he does. But if we dig a little bit deeper, we will find love, no matter how hard a person may look on the outside. When we dig deeper, we encounter the soul, and the soul is made of a gentle substance we call love.

Every time we feel love, that love stays with us. That experience will never disperse. Each experience of love accumulates in us and becomes part of us. The more love we experience, the more loving we become. We carry this accumulated love with us from lifetime to lifetime until we become one with Existence. Then we are total love.

Love needs to be renewed all the time, otherwise it becomes just a dead memory. But even that memory can be essential in renewing love.

Love comes in three different forms. The first form is the love between a man and a woman, which is basically a love-hate relationship. This love involves many complicated issues. There are many highs and lows, but these highs and lows help us to grow. The second form is friendship. Friendship can happen between a man and a woman or anyone. Friendship involves a lot of give and take, respect, and caring for one another. The third form of love is compassion. Compassion happens in the higher chakras. Compassion is pure love; it is unity. This love is totally unconditional and has no attachment. It comes with deep understanding and absolute acceptance. Compassion is loaded with lots of good stuff.

The non-duality of our soul is experienced as love. Love means two energies becoming one. This can happen between a man and a woman, two sisters, a mother and a daughter.... The energy of one melts into the energy of the other. Love causes us to become one. When this happens, we join with the existential force and we feel extremely happy. That is love.

The problems that we get from our parents are the issues we have come to this earth to work on. If we did not have any problems, we would not be born. For example, the male usually gets angry; that is the negativity of the male. The female usually withdraws; that is her negativity. It is very important to pay attention to both these patterns in us, because we all have a male and female side of our brain.

There is always a fight between the male and female inside us. They are at war because the male and female don't understand each other. The male hates the female; therefore, the female hates the male. There is a conflict. Of course, it is for our growth. If we don't like someone, if someone is disturbing us, it is only because our male and female inside are disturbed. Then we have problems with people. These problems come from our parents. They had disturbances with each other. If the mother yelled at the father, the inner female is yelling at the inner male all the time. When we watch our outer conflicts, we become more aware of our inner conflicts, and we come to understand our inner male and female more. With this understanding and awareness, we grow beyond the conflicts and our male and female become friends. Imagine, all of this is just for our growth.

Men and women have both male and female energy in them. When things get bad, the female almost always attacks herself. The male always attacks others. If I am a person that puts myself down *and* gets into fights with others, both my male and female are active. If I am ninety percent female, I put myself down ninety percent of the time. If I am ninety percent male, I put others down ninety percent of the time. Humans are always some combination of male and female. If I have more female energy, I feel guilty. So the female feels bad a lot. Feeling guilty basically means putting yourself down or condemning yourself. When the male comes up, it condemns others. This is how he protects himself. With love, we can drop this game; then it is possible to create a high-quality human being. By the way, the female's way of protecting herself is putting herself down, so others come to rescue her.

If we are more male or more female, we cannot grow much. Growth happens when, for any reason, the male and female join together. If we think something is our fault, in that moment we are more female, so we cannot grow. If we think it is the other person's fault, we are more male and again we cannot grow. When we go deeper, we go beyond male and female. Then everything is fine. Only on the surface is there duality. Right and wrong exist only on the surface. The same for positive and negative. In the depth there is no positive or negative. There is only the soul. If you look deeper, you cannot find anybody at fault. Everyone is right in a way and love rules.

Everything starts from within. Whatever is outside is just a reflection of our inside. So getting mad at others or wanting to change them is totally irrelevant. We need to heal ourselves and the outside will change accordingly. Getting mad at ourselves also doesn't do anything for us. The only thing that helps is love. Pain, bad memories, and wounds are okay because they can all be healed if we keep giving love. How do we love? By becoming aware. Becoming more aware that I am getting upset. That brings love. Becoming more aware that I am not happy right now. That also brings love. Awareness means bringing love. When we are not happy, it means *we* are not giving love or we are not bringing awareness. If we were giving love, we would be happy. It is as simple as that.

The female always wants sweets and sugar because sugar makes her male stronger. The fourth chakra, the heart chakra, is all about love and sweetness. Sugar represents the sweetness of love, and the female is all about love. Sugar makes fire, which is a male element, within us. So someone with a strong female side uses sugar to balance herself with this male. Sugar balances this strong female energy and opens the heart. The heart chakra is all about gentleness, but gentleness is softness and strength together, so this balance between male and female energy is crucial to totally opening the heart. It seems like I am promoting sugar (laughing). I do not own a sugar factory, so don't think sugar is the only way to open the heart. One kiss will be better than sugar.

The only way we feel deserving in life is when we have love. If we have love, we feel we deserve to have nice things, good relationships or money. Love is the only way. Even if we have a good relationship, if we don't feel deserving, we will ruin it. If we have money, but we don't feel deserving, that money will only bring problems and unhappiness to us. It is only a deep feeling of deserving that makes everything we have work for us. It makes life sweet. We like our life and we have acceptance for things. This deserving energy also creates a positive energy field around us that affects those with whom we come into contact. People change around us because of this positive energy. Their relationship with us changes for the better.

If our female side feels weak, then we feel undeserving. The only way to make our female strong is with love. Then our male side feels this love and gets attracted to our female and he becomes stronger. In fact, they become balanced—the male and the female. Love balances the energies of male and female inside us. They become one and we go to our soul, which is beyond these two opposites. We feel ecstatic. Anytime we feel love, we move to our soul, and we experience a deep feeling of happiness and bliss.

Love originates from within, but then it flows outward and we feel it. It can happen when we watch a sweet movie or when we experience gentleness in a connection with someone. Both love *for* the outside and love *from* the outside trigger the love of our inner female. Then lots of healing for our body and soul happens. This love brings us happiness, aliveness and youth. The only healer in Existence is love.

The male and female outside are only a reflection of our inner male and female. The way others treat us is the way our own inner male and female treat each other. The male has power and control, but love comes from the inner female and love is everything. Love is higher than control. The female just needs to recognize her strength. To become strong, the female only has to gain the wisdom of knowing herself and the power of love. The male is strong; he can either crush the female or he can be at the service of the female and help her flourish. When he supports the female, we can be successful in every aspect of our lives—in happiness, in joy, in love, in health, in money-making, in life as a whole. It is all up to the love of the female.

When we have problems with someone, like our husband or wife, it only shows that our own inner male and female are having problems with each other. In a woman, for example, if her female is weak, it gets dominated by her male and she falls apart. Furthermore, her inner male gets reflected onto her husband or some other outer male, and he becomes demanding because the male inside her is demanding. Facing this outer male, the female gives in. We call this repression, and it leads to unhappiness and misery. The female doesn't like this dominating male, and the male doesn't like the female because a weak female pouts and nags and is easily upset. It makes the male frustrated, and he wants to crush her.

The female needs to become strong, but strong doesn't mean tough; it means loving. Only the female side of us can love. Our male side doesn't have love. It can only have power or be weak. If the female is happy, loving, and accepting of the male, the male feels accepted and becomes accepting in turn. If not, he wants to fight. With acceptance, the male and the female can merge, creating happiness and enjoyment. The only reason people are unhappy is because their inner male and female are always in conflict. If we understand our male and female more deeply, they get healed and we have a joyful life.

When our inner male and female come together, our outer relationships will get healed too. Love is so strong that when it happens, it wipes out every pattern or problem from the past. Love cleanses everything. Love has power. When the female loves, the male joins in. When the female is loving, which is the female at its most mature level, then love will rule in the household. We just have to love the male, so the male opens up and joins the female.

The mind says, "That person didn't look at me right. They must hate me. I knew it!" We get upset because we want the space to be loving. We want to love and be loved. The female always wants to connect and love. When she feels there is no love, she withdraws to protect herself. She says, "I'm not going to talk to you anymore. I'm going to close myself." She does all this because she wants to love and be loved, but she doesn't know how to go about it. Her inner male is not helping. We need these two opposite energies, male and female, to come together in order to have harmony inside. This harmony leads to understanding. When we do not understand the subtleties of life, we become very superficial. We often close ourselves and are phony. We smile because we do not know what else to do. But our real intention is to love.

    Personally, I look at life more deeply and I respect and love everyone, even people who close themselves. Recently, I went to a store and the clerk had a very negative attitude. I know she has love; she just doesn't know how to show it. She was nasty in that moment, but I love her anyway. Always remember that, just like you, everyone wants to love and be loved. We just don't know how to go about it.

The female wants love. All of her expectations come from wanting love. If we go deeper into any expectations, we will get to love. Always when we go deeper into anything, we get to love. And when we go deep in love, we reach the soul. If we go deep into the soul, we reach the universe.

Most of the time, our expectations do not get fulfilled. Then we fall apart; we get angry or sad. If we don't expect, we appreciate everything that happens. It makes us happy. If we can let go of our expectations, we won't get frustrated anymore. We won't fall apart. We won't dislike. We just go with the ways of God and live a happy life.

When we have expectations of others, they do not like it and resist. If our expectations go on for a long time, they will start hating us. Really, expectation is the opposite of love, because love does not expect anything.

The mind feels safe when everything is planned. It does not know that things only become fun and exciting when they happen spontaneously. When we do not expect, we come to the moment, and when we come to the moment, everything is fun.

Expectation always makes our experiences weaker because it keeps us in the mind. The mind goes to old memories. These memories don't allow us to be in the moment and to experience what is. All experiences happen when we think less, so being in the moment is crucial for having new experiences. When we are not in the moment, we are just in the illusion of all the past memories residing in the mind's memory cells. When something happens without our expectation, it always becomes stronger, tastier.

With expectation, life is a drag. When we don't expect, whatever happens is so much fun. When we expect, we become entitled. Then, if what we expect doesn't happen, we fall apart; but if it happens, it is not as much fun anymore because we expected it to happen. And in the meantime, we are always worried that our expectations might not be met. Worrying is misery. Expect anything and you will be miserable all the time. Expectation gets us in each and every way.

When we expect something of someone, it is almost like we are being their enemy, because love never expects anything. And every time we are upset with anyone, if we look at it more deeply, we will see that it is because we have certain expectations of them. So, basically love means having no expectation.

Love heals our male and female energy inside.
So love others and you will be healed.

Healing happens when we totally trust. But if even for a moment we think, "I am being negative and people don't like negativity," our trust goes away. Any judgement, either of ourselves or others, creates fear and we close ourselves. The slightest fear, worry, or lack of trust and the fifth chakra, the chakra dealing with trust, closes. With a closed fifth chakra, we cannot express ourselves, so healing cannot happen. We stay closed. Then, the miracles that come with trust don't happen, for example, transformation doesn't happen. Our issues and problems remain until we gain a deeper understanding of them and ourselves. Understanding helps us to trust again. Understanding happens when the fourth chakra, the heart, and the third chakra, the mind, come together. When understanding happens, love happens, closeness happens, unity happens, yumminess happens, and healing happens.

Expressing feelings happens through the fifth chakra. To be able to express, one has to have the fifth chakra functioning. The essence of this chakra is male, so people with a healthy fifth chakra usually have a healthy relationship with their father, because our father is our original source of male energy on the outside. When the fifth chakra is open, we trust more, and we need trust to be open and express ourselves. Expressing our feelings is essential. People who cannot express themselves become sarcastic and angry. Those who didn't have a healthy relationship with their father can create a healthy fifth chakra by trusting someone who can guide them through life with wisdom and love. If we can trust one person totally, we can trust the whole of Existence.

As we sing, we bring energy to our throat chakra. The fifth, or throat chakra is about trusting—trusting ourself and the whole universe. So singing makes us feel more trust. When we trust, lots of blessings open up for us. Existence opens the door of plentitude in our lives. There will be an abundance of love, happiness, money—everything. Singing truly changes people's lives. All joy comes from our soul and singing brings us to our soul. Our mind doesn't make us happy—the soul always makes us happy. The mind is a tool, but the real deal comes from our soul. We can do a lot of things in our life, but for really high quality, it has to come from the soul. So, sing and hug yourself!

The third chakra is male. It is about winning, controlling, success, and making things happen. All of these show a lack of trust and bring us anxiety. The fourth chakra is more female and feels love. Only by trusting Existence can we get to the fourth chakra. The more we trust, the more we move from the third chakra to the fourth. In the fourth chakra there is love and let go.

There is healthy seriousness and unhealthy seriousness. When there is obsession in seriousness, then it is unhealthy. Obsession means bringing our fear into a situation. With fear we lack trust and therefore want to control. We become attached to certain outcomes and even how we are going to get to those outcomes. With a deeper understanding of Existence, obsession leaves and we become playfully serious. And that is perfect. Two opposite poles, playfulness and seriousness, meet and a higher quality happens. An enlightened person is playfully serious. Why? Because he/she totally trusts Existence. Acceptance means trust. Acceptance takes the obsession out of seriousness. So acceptance is a healing force that makes us free from obsession, and when we are not obsessed, we are not attached to a specific goal or outcome. Goals are a part of obsession. Planning is fine. We plan, but we go with whatever Existence wants. We do not get attached to results. We do not worry about it. If Existence wants, it goes with our plan, and if it does not want, it doesn't go with our plan. Existence is perfect. We don't need to worry. We just have to trust. When we begin to understand how beautifully organized everything is by Existence, we see how immature it is for us to sit there and worry. Our job on this planet is to go beyond the immaturity of the mind.

When we are total, we cannot be serious. It is only when we are not total that we become serious. Seriousness means the conscious and the unconscious minds are working against each other. They are fighting one another, and anytime we have an inner fight, we lose energy. Someone who is serious, then, loses a lot of energy and therefore suffers. We think of these people as dry or cold. When we are playful, our conscious and unconscious minds are in agreement and we feel calm. We do not need to be enlightened to be playful and calm. We just need totality. If we want something with all our being, seriousness goes away. We become playful. When we control, we worry that something might happen in the future that we won't like. So we are unhappy that we might be unhappy at some point in the future. In this way, we worry and are for the most part unhappy. But the truth is, these bad things we worry about rarely happen. So it really makes sense to not be upset now because we might be upset later.

People often ask me, is everything predetermined? It is not "pre." Everything gets determined as we go along. It's just determined, not pre-determined. As you go along, life happens. Everything gets determined, not by us but by Existence. And there is really no us. By existing, we are Existence. So whatever *we* do, Existence is doing. We are Existence trusting that Existence is running the show. We feel the unity, and we love everyone and everything. If we don't trust, we cannot love. Only when you trust Existence is love possible.

Existence is all about sharing. If we share with others, Existence shares more with us. Then we can share even more with others. If we don't share, why would Existence share with us? If we are not sharing with others, Existence thinks we must have enough since we are keeping everything for ourselves. Then more won't come. This is why business is so rewarding, because it is about sharing. You hire people to work for you, you share with them and Existence shares with you. Therefore, it is so successful. That is why even in the world, people like business because it is a mystical phenomenon. It is about sharing and love.

Trust helps love grow, and love helps trust grow. As love grows, we feel content and fulfilled. Of course, the mind can always come in and bring negativity again, but our love never goes anywhere. It stays and accumulates.

When someone wants to replace us, it just means we are ready to go higher. We have to let go of where we are to go to a higher place. So someone wanting to replace us is the love of Existence wanting us to let go of where we are and go higher. When we are stuck somewhere and don't want to move, Existence sends someone to pull us out of our rut. If nobody takes our place, we stay where we are. We don't grow. If we have wisdom, we give space to whatever is happening. When we do, we move to a higher level. This is an ancient attitude of the wise.

Fear of rejection is something that most humans feel and is the reason people have become so separated from each other. This feeling is a wound in our emotional body that can be used for our personal growth. It motivates us to work on ourselves. Love is at the heart of this work. The more we feel real love, the more the second and fourth chakras cleanse, which makes it possible for us to feel even more love. Basically, love replaces the wound. With love, we step deeper and deeper into our soul.

If we are being rejected by someone, we have to pay attention to see what the problem is that the other person sees in us and gain more understanding of it. Rejection by others is the love of Existence. Existence is all love; we are love, our body is love, our emotions, our ego. Everything is love. A mystic should know that there is nothing against love. This is why a mystic loves everything.

Working on the self is a very long process, but you don't really go anywhere. The only destination is here and now. There is no goal. Only the mind has goals and if there was a goal in life, we would have achieved it by now. Here is everything. There is only this moment, and whatever is happening right now is our only goal. So just be here and now.

Sometimes, when we come to a new understanding in our life, we feel like we haven't grown at all; that we are back at the very beginning of our path and have a long way to go. But this feeling just shows that we *have* grown. We have come to a new space in our understanding. It is a beginning, but it is a beginning at a higher level. If we feel this way often, it just shows we are growing a lot.

When we grow, we go to a new space and when we go to a new space, there is always chaos. Chaos basically means a new space. If we don't grow, we stay where we are. There won't be any chaos, but there won't be any joy either. When chaos happens, we just need to give ourselves time to get acquainted with this new space.

So growth brings joy, but at the same time it brings fear of the chaos that comes with it. Unconsciously, people know that growth is a little uncomfortable. Because of this, we often resist looking at ourselves, but if we don't grow for a long time, life becomes boring. We become attracted to filth. We become narrow-minded and start misusing others. Not growing for a long time leads to destruction. We can become evil or even kill ourselves.

Chaos and negativity are necessary. They throw us off our center which helps us to grow. Falling apart and becoming centered again is growth. When we use our mind, we become heavy. When we meditate and relax, we let go. Each time we let go, we grow.

Every time we go through hell, we gain heaven. We always gain heaven going through hell. There is a certain deeper maturity we gain every time we go through hell. Opposite poles always go together and enhance each other.

Everything has wisdom. Even our lack of wisdom has its own wisdom. A lack of wisdom puts us in situations that motivate us to gain wisdom and become mature, and this process is wisdom. Existence is impeccable.

When we work on ourselves, we see that problems are just our homework. We don't get upset by them; instead, we gain understanding from them. This we call mysticism.

I look at politics and I love it. The conflict is working. I look at our history and see that conflict has always been there and that it has caused so much growth. Everything has become more refined today, more subtle and advanced, because of conflict. Everything is going towards advancement. It may be slow, but I love it. Why rush? Where do we want to get to? We are here to enjoy whatever happens.

There is one exercise that is very effective in helping a person grow, and that is this: anytime you are doing something, all of a sudden stop doing it for a few seconds. Just freeze and then continue on with your activity. No matter what you are doing, whether it is walking or reading or washing dishes, just stop; pause for a moment. This pause will bring you back to the moment and yourself. If you can do this with your emotions, it is even stronger. For example, if you are angry, just stop your anger for a few seconds. If it's too hard to do it with emotions, do it with any daily activity. This exercise will bring lots of awareness, which always leads to growth.

Everything we do in life is for us to grow. Even our negative thought patterns help us grow. They are a great opportunity because we pay more attention when we are unhappy or negative. This attention helps us become aware, so our awareness grows. All the problems that the mind makes are challenges for our awareness. The pain that negativity creates is a great opportunity for growth, because in pleasure, we cannot watch anything. In pleasure, we are busy with enjoying, not awareness.

When someone has a strong male, they do things all the time. The nature of the male is to be active. It cannot settle down. Naturally, such a person struggles to be calm and meditative. If it is time for this person to grow, Existence allows a physical problem to happen that forces the person to reduce their activity. This helps them to settle down. In this way Existence is helping them work on themselves. In becoming less active, they become more female. Balance comes to them. This is the love of Existence.

When we do things, we lose energy. This is because we do things without awareness. If we do things with awareness, we don't lose energy. When we are aware, our unconscious and conscious minds are working together. There is no inner conflict between these opposite sides, so our energy is not wasted.

At times we think "Everything seems so messed up; how can God be at work?" But mysticism means things are the way they are supposed to be, and everything is perfect. We just have to see and understand this deeply. In the material world, if you want to be smart and succeed, you have to turn every opportunity into money. But in the realm of the soul, if you want to be smart and succeed, you have to use every opportunity to become more aware. With awareness, you can be total in any moment regardless of what is happening. We want to become more conscious because the more conscious we are, the less we suffer.

People say God works in mysterious ways. This is true if we are ignorant, but if we become closer and closer to God, we learn to see His ways. Then they are not mysterious anymore. They are simple and fun.

There are three levels of consciousness in humans. The first level is society. Society is the norm by which most people live. It is about appearances and keeps us on the surface of our mind. This level of consciousness is mostly concerned with things, money, and superficial relationships with others. The second level is nature. Nature can mean things like trees, animals, and mountains, but it also means natural tendencies in humans like eating, being attracted to the opposite sex, and survival instincts. We have to move from the society level of consciousness to nature and then from nature to our soul. When we start understanding the soul, we become spiritual.

Love needs awareness to turn to understanding. Love without awareness is just love. Love with awareness becomes a strong insight which we call understanding.

We can divide humanity into two groups: people who are more aware and those who are less aware. When we feel bad about ourselves or worry that others don't like us, the less aware people will fall into our energy and act accordingly. They will have problems with us. The more aware people won't fall into our energy. They are more open and understanding, so they don't judge us.

We need to be aware that the conscious and the unconscious minds work in opposite ways. If we are happy, our unconscious mind is unhappy. If we are unhappy, our unconscious mind is happy. These two always work in opposition to one another. Only when we go beyond all duality do the conscious and unconscious minds become one. How do we go beyond duality? With love, pure acceptance, trust, or any higher quality.

Understanding comes from seeing or looking deeper into things. When we see something deeply, we understand. To figure things out with our mind is not understanding. We can call it mind understanding, which is different from the deep understanding that happens in our Being. Seeing means things become clear. When there is clarity, the mind sees it and thinks that it knows. Then, if we try to explain it to others, there are two possibilities. If we talk entirely from the mind, people get tired of our talking because it gets heavy and we feel like we are talking too much. If we talk from understanding, it never feels like too much. If we talk from our deeper understanding, which is beyond the mind, we can talk for hours and nobody gets tired. Everything is incredibly exciting and fun when we see something with deeper understanding.

The language of our soul is silence. The language of the mind is words. The only way we can have a deep understanding is by combining the words of the mind with the silence of the soul. How do we hear the silence of the soul? Our heart has to open. When we go deeper, we pass the noises of the mind, which are on the surface, and immediately our whole energy moves to the heart center. When the door to the heart opens, you have the words of silence. Then we use the mind only to communicate with the soul. When the mind stops, any negativity like expectation, jealousy, wanting to put people down, or old memories, stop. The mind becomes a powerful force that can experience the here and now, which *is* the heart center, or pure joy. When we have the silence of the soul and the words of the mind together, understanding comes. When these two languages combine, we have understanding, which leads to love.

When two people meet with their minds, there is no energy. They meet in deadness. There is no life in the mind: it's just a bunch of dead rules, memories, judgments, feeling not good enough, fear of criticism, and doubts. It is a mess. When we feel love or listen to music and are totally absorbed in it, there is no mind. Our energy comes alive, and we are totally in the joy of our soul. We are alive.

The only time we can give space is when we are calm. With a busy mind comes stress. Then we cannot give space to anyone, even ourselves. We push people away. Only someone with a calm and empty mind can give space to themselves and others.

If we are ambitious, we want to be better than others. If others are also ambitious, we don't like it because they also want to be better than us. We don't like that they want to be better than we are. But if we authentically believe that we are the best, then it will be fun to watch people compete with us. It is very interesting how ego works.

The mind is always in search of great power because it feels inferior. Somewhere along the way somebody yelled at us and told us, "You are not good. You are good for nothing." It only takes one time hearing this for us to believe it. And then we spend our whole lives trying to prove to ourselves that we are good.

Jealousy comes from guilt, because guilt says, "I am no good," "I am worthless," or "I don't deserve because I have done something wrong or am a bad person." If I am unworthy, I feel guilty having something that I am not worthy of, like a good life, or nice things or a loving relationship. And if I am worthless, I feel jealous when someone else is worthy, either in my eyes or another's eyes. If I didn't feel guilty, I wouldn't feel jealous, and there would be no competition. Guilt and jealousy create all kinds of competition, some subtle and some not so subtle. You might not even know that you are competing. For example, imitation is a form of competition. When you imitate, you think this person is better than I am, so I better act or be like them. Imitation is a form of jealousy. This all comes from feeling guilty and inferior. Inferiority complexes can come from guilt and even create guilt. The good news is that love is the remedy. It heals all wounds. Love fixes any negativity: inferiority complexes, jealousy, competition, comparison.

The mind has a certain outlook or perspective with which it looks at everything. The source of this perspective is perfectionism. When we look at things through the perspective of the mind, we only see the negative, not the positive. If we look at ourselves, we only see our problems and not our advancements. It is very important to pay attention to this. It is the love of Existence that we can't see our advancements because it stops our ego from taking credit for them. But it is good to occasionally see how far we have come because it motivates us to keep moving forward in our growth.

Acceptance basically means not being a perfectionist. Perfectionism is against acceptance. If we think things need to improve and become better, then wherever we are, we do not accept. We will dislike many things around us, because we think they are not perfect as they are. If we go beyond perfectionism and know that everything is perfect the way it is, all of a sudden we have acceptance. We will do our best in whatever we do, but we will not be obsessive about it. We understand that everything is the way it is supposed to be. All we need to remember is that everything is perfect the way it is.

The only person doubting if you are lovable or not is you. Because you doubt, you send a message out to others, through a subtle vibration of energy that says, "I am not lovable." This energy creates a subtle separation in others' minds. They love you, but they also get this message that you are not lovable. They love you on one hand, and on the other, they feel they don't love you and they don't know why. They start thinking you did something wrong. If you don't send this message out, nobody doubts you. People love you totally. It is always us doing it, not somebody else. Understanding this is total maturity.

If someone has not been loved, their mind becomes negative. They may not even know they are negative. This is what doubt is. Mind doubts all the time because of all the negativity in the memory cells of the brain. The heart trusts. When we surrender to Existence, which means no complaining, no disliking anything, accepting whatever is, a higher quality happens to us. That quality is trust and when we trust, immediately we feel love. Love is the quality of our soul. When the heart is full of energy, immediately we love.

The job of the mind is to bring negativity into everything and make that negativity bigger and bigger. If we go with the game of the mind, we become old, angry, and negative. Understanding transforms negativity to positivity and then it moves us beyond these dualities. The positive is just the other side of the negative; what we really want is to go to the Beyond. With understanding, negativity becomes a cleansing experience that helps us grow and reach the Beyond. Every time we are in the Beyond, we feel love. And every time we feel love, we become fresh and young. We just need to bring understanding into every situation. When we do this, we are in the Beyond all the time.

Mental and emotional wounds are just negative memories. The nature of the mind is to be negative and bitter, so all our negative memories get stuck there. It is our job to become aware of our wounds and negative memories and work on them. When we do this sincerely, then every day that passes, we find a new maturity. At first, it may feel like we aren't getting anywhere, that every day is just like the first day and our wounds are the same as always, but each day we get a little more mature. Over time, as our maturity continues to grow, our wounds become easier to overcome. Every day Existence gives us a deeper ability to understand. Every time we sleep at night, we do a jump. The next morning, we have more capacity for deeper understanding. Finally, one day, all the wounds will subside. All the negative memories will disappear.

There are three types of orgasm in humans and they all lead to the same place. There is the physical orgasm of which we are all aware. With this orgasm, the mind stops and we feel loved. There is also a mental orgasm. The mental orgasm follows the physical orgasm and happens when the mind stops. There is also an emotional orgasm. The emotional orgasm happens when we feel touched by something, for example art or music. For a moment our breathing stops. The beauty takes our breath away and again, the mind stops. When the mind stops, the energy of the mind goes entirely to the heart. Anything that stops the mind causes us to feel love and to feel the moment entirely. Therefore, we can say love is an orgasm.

The reason sex is so appealing is because it gives us a taste of our soul, or the Beyond. As we get closer to orgasm, the mind slows down more and more, and energy that would normally go to the mind moves to the chakras instead. The chakras are the bridge between the body and soul, so when the mind stops, we get a glimpse of our soul, or the Beyond.

The turmoil of the mind never stops. It is always there. The only way to get out of this turmoil is to go deeper. The mind is on the surface. All we need to do is go deeper than the mind. How do we go deeper? Music, love, understanding, acceptance, not resisting, not fighting, meditation, or becoming total in anything we do helps us to go deeper than the mind.

The mind has a very cunning trick. Whenever it is miserable, it makes it other people's fault. We are the victims of this trick because in this way, negativity and misery can never be dropped. They are out of our hands.

Anytime we get hurt or bothered, it is because of our ego. In reality, everything that exists is beautiful. Existence does not make ugliness. Ego may think this person is behaving in an ugly way and that behavior shows they don't love me. But the mind or ego only feels this way because we have been taught that this behavior is something we shouldn't like. The mind is constantly telling us that something is wrong and bad. Society has created a set of rules about how things should be, but in Existence those rules do not exist. Things are the way they are. Everything happens in the moment and everything is beautiful. But ego and mind are always trying to create problems. Every time there is something positive, they find something negative in it. Every time we get upset, we just have to see that the ego is doing its job of making us miserable. If we can see that our being upset is related to our conditionings of right and wrong passed down from society, the ego will stop bothering us. We just have to catch the ego; then it cannot bother us anymore.

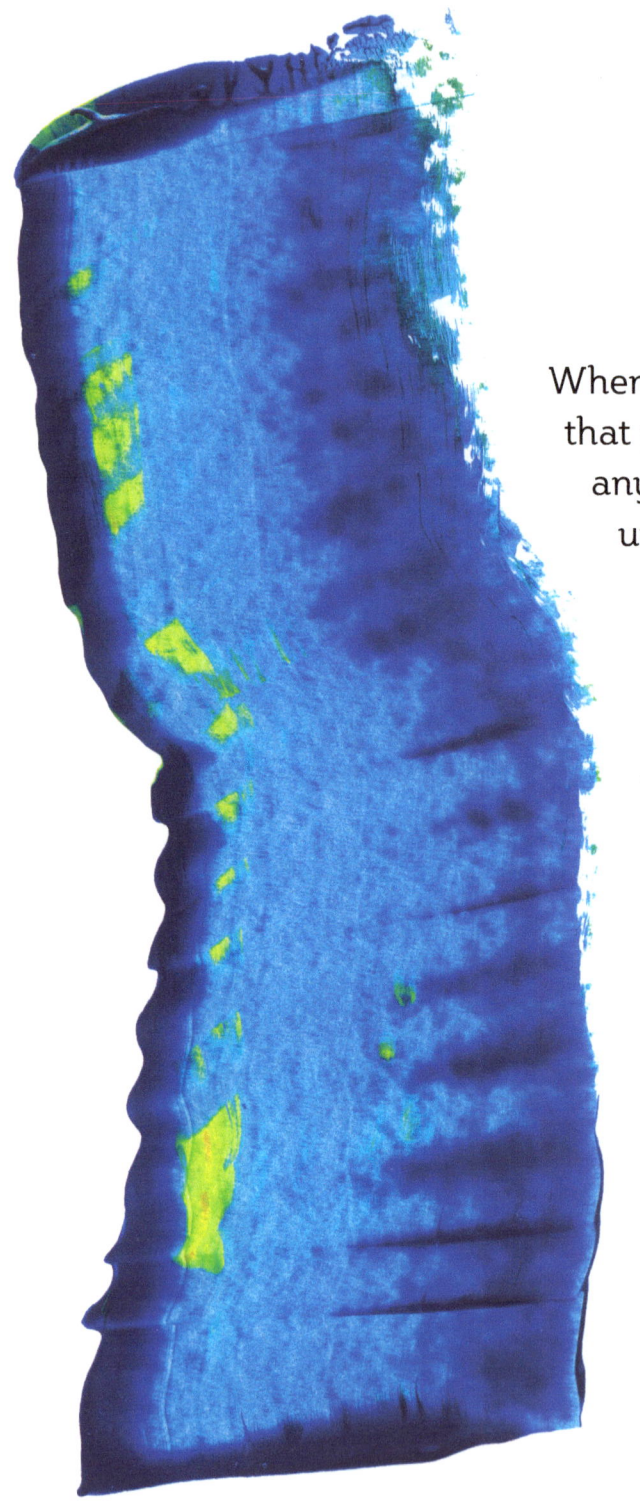

When we treat someone with harshness, that person doesn't feel love for us anymore, which is the same as being unaware. So if we are harsh, people become unaware and respond with negativity and destruction. This is human nature. If we are loving with others, they will be loving and aware with us. If we are working with people, this love will bring harmony and things will fall into place. So to help people do their job well, be loving.

Every time we feel love, the ultimate job of the ego is to separate us and get us out of that feeling of love. Then we try again to go to love, and the ego gets us out again. We cannot stay in love unless we pass a border called enlightenment. Then we can stay in love. The only reason Existence has given us the ego is for it to take us away from love and for us to find our way back to love. This is the service ego has provided us. This going to love and coming out brings us growth. If this love is with a spiritual being, then the growth is much deeper. It creates growth in all the layers of our being. The love sinks in and accumulates.

When we have less ego, we feel deserving of love. Usually, the ego says, "I am better than others, so no one can give me love." The other side of the ego says, "I have no value and I don't deserve love." These two sides are always there together. I am the best and I am the worst. We get confused and caught in this loop. And when we feel we are not deserving, we reject love. When we feel better than others, we feel no one is good enough to give us love. Then also, we reject love.

Ego is our friend but we do not recognize this because we see the ego as negative. It has become our enemy. Ego is our friend because it constantly helps us grow. It is such a great friend that if we have a problem or blockage, it comes in and blows it all out of proportion so it becomes an urgent matter for us to work on. In this way we continue to grow and move forward. One day, when we don't need the ego anymore, it will go away forever.

Fear is the base of the ego. From there, if we go deeper, we move beyond fear. Ego is very superficial. If we go deeper into it, we pass through it to our soul.

We have incorporated many subtle understandings into our lives and the many experiences that have created wounds in us. These wounds make up the dark side of our psyche. We need to understand these wounds and bring light to them. Then we see our wounds vanish by exchanging them with these subtle new understandings. This is the way of Existence.

When we understand that there is no "I," then what remains is oneness. Only unity is. Then we feel love. Love comes from this understanding that there is no "I." There is only oneness with everyone.

In mysticism, a lot has been said about non-doing. Non-doing does not mean not doing anything. It means to do things with totality. When we are total the "I," or the ego, is not there, and because of that, there is no friction inside us. When the "I" is not there, whatever we are doing is basically done by Existence. So what we really mean by non-doing is non-being. Doing happens when some part of us is rejecting another part. We call these two parts the ego. When we are total, we are not there. Totality is Existence.

How can we serve Existence? If we serve our soul, we serve Existence. If we serve the ego, we are serving the ideas of society, which are mostly in opposition to the ideas of Existence. Society is a fake existence that we have created around us. As a mystic, we need to distinguish between the fake and the real thing. Our soul, or the Beyond, is the real Existence. To bring the soul out and allow it to function is to serve Existence.

How close people are depends on their level of understanding and love. A person could be your brother, wife or husband and not be close to you at all, while a person who has no relation, but who has love and understanding, could be very close. So, love and understanding are the measure of closeness.

Always, understanding takes us to our soul, and in our soul, we feel joy.

We can never do anything wrong, because whatever happens is what we need. There is nothing wrong with being wrong, then, because our "wrongs" are what we need for our growth. When we take things seriously, we suffer, but even that is okay because it helps us grow. So it's just fun to be alive and grow.

If we are always worried that we might be wrong, we become passive. Fear of being wrong will cause us to withdraw and be in the background because we are so worried that if we say something, it might be wrong. We might not even be aware of this fear anymore; now we are just automatically passive. This is the nature of a mind that criticizes itself all the time. Whatever anyone says, the mind looks at it from the angle of being right or wrong. There is no alternative.

We have to understand that in every situation there is positive and negative. They are always together and they support each other. The negative has been labeled bad, and therefore wrong, and the positive good or right; but we need both these two forces together to keep us alive. We are like a lamp. A lamp needs both a positive and a negative charge to stay lit. More often than not, the mind finds the negative in every situation, not the positive. When the mind does this, we become passive to avoid the wrong. But positivity and negativity are always together. If we condemn one, we are not seeing the whole picture. We are not looking deep enough. Think of a house. The negative is the base of the house, the positive is the house itself, and the space inside is our soul. These three are always together.

If we have a sensitive mind that is geared towards positivity, we always look at the positive and are assertive. If we have a sensitive mind that is geared towards negativity, we always see the negative and are passive.

When we are afraid, we repress. Then, we become passive. Fear is the cause of passivity. And what fear are we talking about? The fear of judgment, both self-judgement and the judgement of others. We judge ourselves, and we worry that others will judge us if we are not perfect. For example, if we come out and assert ourselves, people might criticize us; better to be quiet or passive and maintain our illusion of perfection. When we are perfectionists, we feel worthless inside. To hide this, we try to show the world that we are perfect. So a perfectionist hates criticism. If we feel worthwhile, we will not be perfectionists and will accept criticism easily.
Feeling worthwhile means we have love. Love is the only true measure of value. If we don't have love, or think that we don't have love, then we feel worthless. But the fact is everyone has a certain amount of love; otherwise, they wouldn't be alive. We are one with God and God is love, so we do have love and therefore value; we just don't know it. Because of this, we substitute perfection for love, and we become passive/aggressive. And just a reminder: if we were perfect, maybe no one would criticize us, but it is impossible to be perfect.

People who are perfectionists become passive, repressive and fearful. They are afraid of others' judgment, so they repress all the time. They usually become sad and depressed because of repression. They try not to express themselves, for fear of others' judgement, and they often end up with physical problems because of the pressure they place on themselves.

Considering others is very important, but it is just as important to consider ourselves. If we only think about others and not ourselves, we become a repressive person. Repression causes our chakras, which are the centers of our etheric body, to get blocked. Then energy does not flow through our etheric body anymore. The etheric body connects the soul to the physical body through the chakras. Each chakra is connected to specific glands in the body that are crucial for our well-being. When the chakras get plugged, then energy can't flow to our physical body. It becomes weak and ill. So we have to be as considerate of ourselves as we are of others. The only way to do this is to express ourselves in subtle and gentle ways that won't offend others, but still inform them about how we feel. People like when others express themselves with openness. It is so refreshing and brings people closer. It is freeing for both sides. When we express gently, it becomes a win-win situation.

When someone dies, it is because their body lacks energy. So the body dies, but the soul goes to the Beyond. Then the soul comes back from the Beyond and is given a new body full of energy. The birth process is painful for the child, but that pain is necessary. It gets rid of a bunch of blockages or karma in the soul from the last life. In this way, the soul becomes more advanced. So with each death, we become more advanced in the next life. Especially if we work on ourselves in this life, then in the next, we will be born into a more advanced and gentle family. This is why there should be no fear of death. We are afraid of death because we get attached to our belongings, family and the people in our lives. We should know that all of Existence is our family and each time we are born, we are given a new family, new toys and friends. It is only the mind that gets attached to things—the mother, father, children, house, etc.—and doesn't want to let them go. We just need to understand that the whole Existence is one with us.

So dying isn't bad, because when we are born again, we will be born into a family that is at the same level as our soul. For example, if we have more love, we will have a very loving family. Not only that, but we will have the abundance of Existence's energy that comes with a new body. This energy will help us grow and jump through a bunch of problems that we were not able to deal with in the last life. Then, we will start learning new things that we need in order to continue to grow on our journey.

People who
get sick and suffer
before they die are cleansing a
lot of karma from this life. When they go on to
their next life, they will be lighter and cleaner. They will be reborn in a
more advanced family. So that pain and suffering are a blessing. They
are the love of Existence. We have always been taught that pain is bad,
so we cannot see the wisdom of it. We create our own suffering by not
having understanding, love, and wisdom. Existence is all about love
and helps us all the time. So pain is cleansing, but fear of death is the
opposite of cleansing. Fear is never cleansing, but it too is necessary.

When we cry, we cleanse our emotional body. We might be conscious of it or not, but nevertheless, we cleanse. When we are more aware, we do not create so much garbage in the emotional body that needs cleansing, so we do not cry much, but if we cry a lot, it is fine. People who cry are actually much more advanced than people who look like they are centered and fine, but who are in fact just not in contact with their emotional bodies. Instead of crying, these people end up with all kinds of sickness and disease. If they could cry, they would cleanse, and their bodies would not get so ill. Today crying does not happen as much. People think they should not cry because it is childish and weak. Everybody tries to control their crying because society teaches us to control it. As a result, there is so much disease and mental problems. Crying makes us fresh. We become young. Those who don't cry, don't cleanse their emotional, mental and physical bodies. They become old and ugly; they always have a sour face and are unhappy. People who cry become fresh, young and happy.

Our vital energy of kundalini gets stimulated by walking or exercise, but that energy gets used by our muscles for the walking or exercise. When we feel love, kundalini energy comes up from the first chakra without getting used for movement of the body. This energy goes to our chakras instead, and from there it pours into our endocrine glands, helping them work at their optimum level. This is why love brings youth and health to a person.

Love gives you juice. It gives you vital energy to expand your chakras. This makes your endocrine glands stronger. Glands are in the physical body, but each gland is next to one of our chakras in the etheric body. So love brings energy to all the chakras and makes us happier and stronger.

When we pay attention to our inner male and female, we gradually begin to understand them. This understanding causes energy to go to our male and female and creates an intensity in them. They become condensed and balanced. Then, this condensed energy moves to our chakras. When it moves to the fifth chakra, it becomes trust and understanding. In the fourth chakra, it becomes love. Sometimes it goes to the sixth chakra and creates miracles.

This process can also happen with acceptance. Acceptance means bringing energy to the male and female simultaneously. A positive person accepts, and their acceptance brings extra energy to their chakras and makes them healthy. So positivity makes you healthy.

People who are negative can become very unhealthy. Negativity takes a lot of energy. With negativity, our chakras become depleted and we become ill. When there is no energy in the chakras, the body dies. Dying means the chakras are not functioning anymore due to all the karma that is plugging them, and karma is created by negativity.

Understanding brings acceptance, and acceptance brings joy and health. When they say your immune system is low, basically it means your chakras do not have enough energy. Chakras are the source of bio-electricity in the body. Positivity and happiness enhance our electricity; negativity depletes us of it. This is mysticism in a nutshell.

When we are angry, we are lacking acceptance. If we bring acceptance to whatever is happening in the moment, we won't be angry anymore. Acceptance comes from understanding. Understanding comes when we are total, when we are totally focused on whatever is happening in the moment. When we are total, our energy goes to our heart, and in the heart, acceptance happens and anger subsides.

When we don't accept, we fall apart. But there is still something we can do. If we cannot accept, we can accept that at this moment we are not accepting. Then we will fall apart anyway, but this time we will do it with acceptance. Our falling apart becomes total and we go through it more easily.

Love helps us become total. When the energy of love is in a space and we are aware of it, we do not want to be anywhere else. We are not conflicted, so we become total in whatever we are doing. One of the ways to become one hundred percent in whatever we do is to be in the presence of love energy. If there is no love in the space, we become partial; part of us does not want to be there. So in pure love, we become one hundred percent and whatever we do becomes powerful and transformative.

When we are total, we are not wishy-washy! Total means not feeling guilty and being absolutely certain about what we are doing. Totality says, I am doing this and it is the only thing I should be doing. Right now, there is nothing else that is important. So when we become total, we are effective. When we are wishy-washy, we are not effective. Some part of us wants to do this thing, but another part does not like it. It is the same with understanding. When we are total, understanding comes and transforms us, but when we are wishy-washy, our understanding becomes partial. Partial understanding is better than no understanding; it still makes us feel good, but it will not transform us nor the issue on which we are working.

When we do something that we consider good, there is more possibility that we can become total in it, because there is no friction in us while we are doing it. We are not worried about it being bad. But there could still be other elements keeping us from being total. For example, if we are in a rush, the feeling of rushing acts as a force that goes against what we are doing and creates friction. Or we could be thinking of something else. Or maybe we are fighting with someone inside our head. These also keep us from being total in our doing. An act that is total has no ego in it. It is basically done by Existence.

Usually, the body rushes because the mind is rushing. You keep thinking you do not have enough time. You have to run. Then the body starts rushing and becomes tense. When we rush, our energy is being used intensively for the mind and body. To be calm, collected and peaceful, our energy has to go to the heart center. When a lot of energy is being used for speed, all of a sudden, there is no energy for calmness and peacefulness. The conscious mind likes to be peaceful, calm and happy, but in this day and age, because we rush so much, we do not have enough energy to be happy and calm. With the pressure that comes from rushing, the conscious mind begins to think something is wrong. It sends a message to the mind saying something is wrong, something is not right. Then, with the slightest provocation, the mind easily falls apart. This is why people are easily upset when they are in a rush. We just need to distance ourselves from this whole phenomenon. We need to become an observer of our rushing and not just in a rush all the time. Then we can be in a rush and it won't bother us. We will have full acceptance for it. If we can be a witness to our rushing, we can rush without losing energy.

Habit means we constantly do something over and over. With habits, we go into a sort of autopilot mode. We can do this habitual thing while our mind keeps busy thinking about other things. It doesn't need to be with the thing we are doing. For example, we drive home from work every day, so we don't need to think about it. We can talk to our friends or think about other things, while the habitual part of the mind gets us home. When we do something that we have never done before, we get out of our minds and come to the moment. Anytime we get out of the mind, we experience the moment. When we laugh deeply or we get scared, we come to the moment. We are not operating from the mind anymore. Also, when we get surprised, the mind stops. That is why we like to surprise people, because they come out their minds and experience deep happiness.

    Witnessing also separates us from the mind and keeps us in the moment. Witnessing means functioning from our soul, but awareness is required to witness. To increase our awareness, we can do certain exercises like drinking tea with awareness and walking with awareness. With witnessing, the mind cannot affect us anymore.

Most of the efforts that we make are done unconsciously because they come out of our habits. To break these unconscious habits, we have to do something that we usually don't do. And it has to be done consciously. When we focus on this conscious effort, all of a sudden our focus becomes total, and totality means going beyond effort. Then our activities become a meditation because the mind stops. When we are total in anything, the mind stops and our soul, or Existence, takes over. All effort on our part stops.

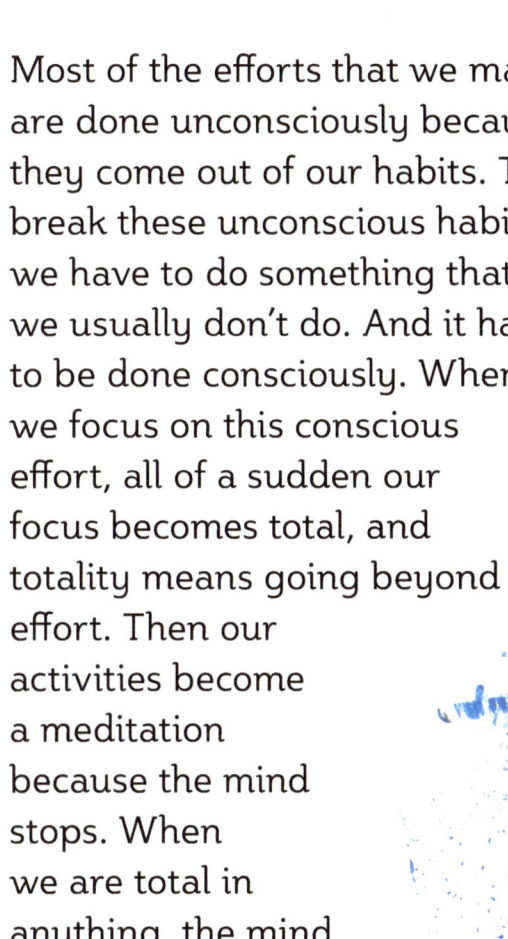

The reason we cannot get out of grief is because we don't accept it. We reject it. We have to accept our grief. Acceptance is a healing force. It does miracles. Acceptance creates totality and when we become total in sadness, at one point we jump out of it. It becomes a huge cleansing. It is beautiful.

When we go beyond something, it doesn't mean that thing doesn't happen anymore. It simply means that if it happens, it is okay and if it doesn't, it is okay. Either way you're happy. But if you are really attached to something happening, you have not gone beyond it yet.

Acceptance comes in two ways, with understanding and/or trust. If we are sensitive and feel things deeply, but we don't have the deeper understandings that lead to acceptance, this sensitivity could be hurtful. In this case, seeing the subtleties in things could make us a negative person. But if we have a deeper understanding and the acceptance that comes with it, then seeing the subtleties or being sensitive becomes an opportunity to grow.

Every time we understand, we drop limiting ideas from our childhood. And, like love, understanding never disappears. It stays with us. It settles in us. It never gets lost. It is good to love and be loved, because it settles in us and adds up. Understanding is the same.

The moment we accept something, we understand it. The reverse is also true, the moment we understand, we accept. We cannot have understanding with rejection. That is why the mind cannot understand, because it is so negative. With negativity understanding does not happen. Only acceptance or positivity leads to understanding. This is the reason why the whole world has such a hard time finding deeper understanding: because the mind is so negative and people are mostly in their minds. Because of the mind, there is a lack of trust, so much judgment and all kinds of negativity. How can anyone understand anything?

Somebody smiles and we think of all the great things they have done and how nice they are. When they frown, we remember how horrible they have been in the past. We feel hurt and a wound is touched inside. Everybody has a good part and a bad part. This is looking at life from a higher view. It helps us to be more accepting and aware when we remember that these two sides exist in everyone.

There is only one way to bring acceptance to all problems and that is to know that anyone who exists is a part of Existence, and Existence, which works through us, doesn't do anything without a reason. Existence always has a higher reason for everything. Something may look lower to us, but that is why they say God works in mysterious ways.

Paintings by Sharam
View and purchase giclée prints

Visit:
TaliaFriends.org

www.ingramcontent.com/pod-product-compliance
Lightning Source LLC
Chambersburg PA
CBHW041550220426
43666CB00002B/27